The Magna Carta Story
The Layman's Guide

Ann Marie Thomas

Best wishes
Ann Marie

Feb 2020

Alina Publishing
Swansea

Published by Alina Publishing
45 Rhondda Street, Mount Pleasant
Swansea SA1 6ER

ISBN: 978-0-9571988-5-2

Printed by CreateSpace

Available from Amazon.com, CreateSpace.com and other retail outlets
Available on Kindle and other devices

Illustrations by Carrie Francis
UndergroundOverground@aol.com

Praise for previous history books:

Ann Marie Thomas has collected together the back story of this tragic figure from Swansea's past. A fascinating account of what really happened in a local landmark many, many years ago...

(Swansea Life magazine)

Though this piece of writing is based on facts, I couldn't help sense a bit of a storyline. Sometimes non fiction can get too caught up in story telling that the underlying facts are put on the backbench but I must stress that while there is an interesting storyline to this piece, the emphasis is on the facts - which is needed in any good non fiction writing. It is a great short piece. The amount of information isn't overwhelming and certainly a good introduction for anybody wanting to research this particular era... it is a wonderful piece that is rich with historical information. It is in fact a great starting point for further research into this field.

(Thomas Falco for Readers Favourite)

We "know" King John. He upset his barons and had to sign Magna Carta. We know little more. This well-written book fills a big hole in history. It explains how their discontent was fueled by his treatment of the lords of Gower and Swansea. Betrayal and intrigues that make the doings of the Ewings pale into the shade. It is presented in an easy-to-read fashion interesting to young and old. A must-have book.

(Bob Woodward)

Broken Reed: The Lords of Gower and King John reads as easily as any novel of political intrigue. Ann Marie Thomas has a way of telling this tale that captures the reader's emotions and sympathies as much as it relates the facts of this transitional period in history. The well-researched facts are easy to follow and the book will quickly become a page-turner to anyone who is intrigued by the political movements of the nobles of that period. Full of intrigue and a solid piece of historical work, Broken Reed: The Lords of Gower and King John is proof that Ann Marie Thomas has established herself in a role that blends historical fact with a knack for storytelling.

(Bil Howard for Readers Favourite)

Contents

Introduction

June 2015 is the 800th anniversary of Magna Carta. Over the centuries it has passed into legend as marking the dawn of democracy.

Let me tell you a secret: At the time, it was no such thing.

The barons had had enough of King John riding roughshod over everyone, and finally gained enough support to threaten him. He reluctantly agreed to the barons' demands and, after some negotiation, set his seal to them.

Another secret: King John didn't sign the charter – he couldn't write, he had people to do that for him. So all the pictures like that above, are inaccurate!

So the barons had brought the king to heel, and democracy dawned, yes?

No. John had already written to the pope about what his barons were trying to do to him, and within a few weeks the pope absolved him from any compliance at all.

But Magna Carta was enforced when John died, and that was the dawn of democracy and rights for all.

No. Democracy was only for 10 percent of the people. Magna Carta is specifically for freemen. Most of the population were serfs and had no rights, and the majority of the charter did not apply to women.

So what's all the fuss?

The fuss is really about the idea that the king is not above the law. This was the first time the king's power was reined in. Until then, 'the divine right of kings' had prevailed, which meant kings could do anything they wanted. Previous kings had had some respect for their subjects, even though they often treated them badly. King John used his subjects for his own ends, and paid the price. Magna Carta made sure (when it was eventually enforced) that no king would ever do the same.

Chapter 1 - King John's Background

Francis
08/13

John was born on Christmas Eve 1166, the youngest child of Henry II and Eleanor of Aquitaine, a powerful woman in her own right. Henry II was the founder of the Plantagenet dynasty of English kings. The last of the line was Richard III whose body was dug up in a Leicester car park in 2012.

In medieval times noble families were not like families today. Babies were handed over to wet-nurses, who usually became their nannies and looked after them for many years. The family structure was not about parents and children as a unit, but about heirs to carry on the line. As the youngest child, John would have expected nothing – no lands or inheritance, hopefully just enough revenue from the king to live on. Another option was to go into the church.

Eleanor of Aquitaine was more involved with her children than was usual at the time, but she took a dislike to John, perhaps because he was conceived on one of Henry's brief infrequent visits. John's three older brothers, Henry, Richard and Geoffrey, had spent much time in childhood with both their parents, but for some reason John was packed off to Fontevraud Abbey at the age of three for five years, leading historians to suggest he was maladjusted.

Today it's thought he had mental health problems or even

suffered autistic spectrum disorder. One commentator said, '*When all allowances for the bias of hostile witnesses have been made, what remains is a clear indication of manic-depressive behaviour, bipolar affective disorder ... – a diagnosis that would account for the violent mood swings and tempestuous rages*'. All of which goes a long way to explaining his unpredictability and bad behaviour as an adult.

Henry II was the overlord of the Angevin empire — he was lord of more land in France than the King of France himself, Louis VII. From their original land of Anjou, his territory stretched all the way from the Scottish border and Ireland to the Pyrenees mountains south of France.

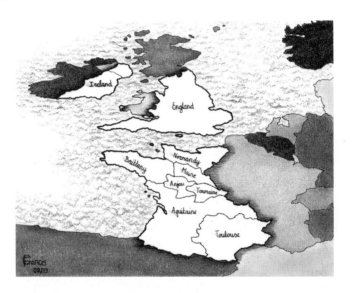

The trouble was, he had so much land, he spent all his reign trying to hold it, waging war in places like Brittany, Normandy, Wales, Scotland and even Ireland, as one magnate or another tried to gain more independence or more land. And he was always at odds with the King of France. John would become the last of the Angevin kings, as during his reign all the lands in France were lost.

In an attempt to spread the responsibility for control of his vast lands and to prevent war between his sons after his death, Henry divided the territory between them and had his eldest son crowned during his lifetime, on 24 May 1170. His son was referred to as the

Young King and Henry as the Old King, since they both had the same name. Richard was given Gascony and Poitou and would inherit his mother Eleanor's territory of Aquitaine. Geoffrey was given Brittany. Henry hoped they would rule the empire as a friendly coalition.

However, the move made his three older sons long for power sooner and, encouraged by their mother, they continuously rebelled and tried to seize territory by force. They were supported by several of the English barons and King Louis of France, Henry's old enemy. The Young King died suddenly of fever on 11 June 1183. Geoffrey was riding in a tournament in Paris when he fell and was badly cut up by the horses' hooves. He contracted a fever and died on 19 August 1186. Henry had to rethink his plans for Richard & John.

Things were further complicated by the birth of Geoffrey's son Arthur of Brittany in the March following his death, who was now second in line to the throne – after Richard and before John. Everybody wanted the right to take care of the baby and influence his education. Things were heading towards war between Henry and Philip, the new French king, until the pope sent a message to say Christian troops should be fighting in the Holy Land, not fighting each other. They couldn't work out terms for peace so they called a two-year truce.

The truce was extended a few months, but as it was coming to an end Henry fell ill. Richard and Philip refused to believe it and began new attacks as soon as the truce ended. As castle after castle fell, Henry was forced to flee and eventually had to submit, pay homage to Philip and give Richard the kiss of peace. In pain from his fever, and humiliation from his defeat, Henry heard on 5 July 1189 his beloved John had also gone over to the enemy, and sworn fealty to Philip. At this betrayal he lost the will to live, and died the following day.

Richard moved at once to secure his hold on the Angevin empire, and release his mother from her latest captivity, making her temporary Regent until he came to England. The Archbishop of Canterbury crowned Richard in Westminster Abbey on 3 September 1189.

Immediately Richard began making plans to go on Crusade. He had to ensure the security of the kingdom in his absence and raise the vast amount of money he would need to finance the expedition. He named his nephew Arthur of Brittany as his heir, hoping to keep John quiet by showering him with Lordships, titles and revenues.

Richard went on Crusade with a great company. He distinguished himself in fighting and strategy, but coming home it was a different matter. He dismissed most of his men, and travelled incognito with a small party. He was captured by Duke Leopold of Austria in December 1192.

The ransom asked for was 100,000 marks (approx. £36m today - a mark was two thirds of a pound) and various undertakings about marriage and goods. It put an enormous burden not only on England's treasury, but on the people, who gave all they could to raise this huge amount. Once Richard was released he returned to England only briefly and then went to France to secure the Angevin lands. He met with Philip of France, and John, and declared John his heir. But the fighting continued.

In the spring of 1199 Richard moved against the Vicomte of Limoges and the Count of Angoulême. At the siege of Chalus-Chabrol he went to inspect the siegeworks without wearing his armour, and was shot by a crossbow. The wound turned gangrenous, and he died on 6 April. All Richard's contemporaries were shocked and uncertain what to do, where to pledge their loyalty, and who would be the next king.

John had spent the previous five years serving Richard as a soldier. He had won many people to his cause by his apparent reform, including his brother. But he still had to fight for his claim to the throne against Arthur of Brittany and Philip, King of France. He made first for Rouen, where he was invested as Duke of Normandy on 25 April, and then raised an army and razed Le Mans for the treason of supporting Arthur. His mother ensured Aquitaine supported him, so he went to England to secure the crown before turning to the other areas in France which were opposed to him.

He was crowned in Westminster Abbey on Ascension Day, 25 May 1199. On 22 May 1200 at Le Goulet John came to an agreement with King Philip of France – his nephew Arthur would get Brittany, which he would hold as a vassal of John, and John would be a vassal of

Philip for the French lands. It seemed John had settled the succession.

John went from being the youngest son, expecting nothing and nothing expected of him, to King of England and the Angevin empire. His older brothers, and to some extent his father, had set him a bad example of how to be a king. It needed firm control, shrewd distribution of power to the right men in the right places, and cunning to play the political games.

John had a fine mind: he instituted reforms in accounting and founded the English navy, but he was not equipped to rule. He used his position to his own ends with little regard for the rights of others. His barons became more and more exasperated with him, but the first person he fought with was the pope.

Chapter 2 – The Pope and the Prophet

When, in June 1205 Hubert Walter, the Archbishop of Canterbury, died, John was determined his successor would be someone who supported him. He selected John de Gray, Bishop of Norwich. The monks and the bishops in Canterbury both believed they should have a say, and sent representatives to the pope. Then some of the monks elected someone secretly and sent him off to Rome too.

Pope Innocent III declared all the elections invalid and invited the monks sent to Rome to hold an election, but they couldn't agree between their candidate and de Gray. The pope settled the issue at the end of 1206 by selecting a different candidate, Cardinal Stephen Langton.

King John refused to accept him, insisting the king had the right to make the appointment, as had been the case in the past. It didn't help that Langton had been a tutor at the University of Paris, thus linking him with John's bitter enemy, King Philip of France. When the pope consecrated Stephen Langton as Archbishop of Canterbury, John refused to allow him entry to England, threw out the Canterbury monks and seized their estates.

Over the following months several bishops fled the country, and John continued to seize church property, until the pope put England under an interdict. This meant in effect that the church was on strike. No church bells rang, no services were held, no marriages transacted.

Priests were allowed to give the last rites to the dying, but new burial grounds had to be created because the dead couldn't be buried in consecrated ground. Religion was an important part of everyday life, and the people felt it keenly, but John was indifferent.

When the interdict failed to bring John to heel, the pope threatened him with excommunication, a threat eventually carried out in November 1209. John continued to be defiant and, saying that the clergy were no longer doing their job, confiscated their estates and then rented them back to them to look after! He raised over £100,000 (over £53 million today) and saw no reason to submit.

But John had other troubles. An excommunicated king was no longer a Christian, and his Christian subjects no longer owed him allegiance. The pope proclaimed a crusade against him and entrusted it to King Philip of France. Furthermore, because of John's bad behaviour towards everyone, his barons were losing patience with him. More and more were joining the rebels, King Philip of France was raising an army, and the whole realm was in a state of limbo.

Then in late 1212, on a trip to the north, John heard about Peter of Wakefield. Peter was a hermit who was prophesying evil against John. Peter's fame spread, news of his prophecy even reaching France. There was wild talk of deposing John or making him abdicate, of finding a new king.

John had him summoned to hear for himself what Peter had to say. Peter was a simple, illiterate man who lived a lonely, ascetic life. He proclaimed he had a vision that John would have only 14 years as king. He told John that by next Ascension Day, 23 May 1213, his crown would be given to another.

Enraged, John had him locked in a dungeon in Corfe Castle, which immediately turned Peter into a martyr in the minds of the people. When Ascension Day came, John had a day-long party to celebrate the failure of the prophecy. Some said that the day Peter meant was actually the fourteenth anniversary of John's coronation, on 27 May, and when that, too, passed without incident, John took his revenge. Peter and his son were dragged behind horses to Wareham and hanged.

But there is a twist to this tale.

John had finally decided to submit to the pope. His barons were being urged that they no longer needed to obey him as king, and he was worried things were getting out of hand. Peter of Wakefield's prophecy may have also made him nervous.

On the eve of Ascension Day in a solemn ceremony at Winchester Cathedral, John welcomed Stephen Langton as Archbishop of Canterbury, and Langton lifted the excommunication. John then swore on the Gospels to change his ways and pay reparations. Thinking to keep the barons in line, John gave his kingdom to the pope, and received back the authority to rule on the pope's behalf.

So John's crown *was* given to another before Ascension Day! Though John would continue to rule, and soon stopped paying reparations, technically the king of England was the pope.

Chapter 3 – The Rise and Fall of William III de Braose

King John took unfair advantage of all his barons, but it was his treatment of William III de Braose that became the final straw, and is a good illustration of John's unstable and paranoid nature.

William III de Braose, 4th Lord of Bramber, came from a distinguished line of Norman barons, of which he was the pinnacle. No one in the family before or after him had such a vast number of lands or wielded such influence. A favourite of King John, he consolidated the lands earned by his predecessors and gained many more. The greatest of his holdings were in Wales where he was lord over a vast swathe of land across mid and south Wales. Yet his very power and intimacy with the king proved to be his downfall, as John became suspicious of him and turned against him.

The family's interests in England began with the Norman Conquest.

Gillaume de Briouze (d.c.1085) was a companion of William the Conqueror at the Battle of Hastings. The Briouze name comes from their estate in the village of Briouze-Saint-Gervais in southern Normandy. William awarded him estates in conquered England which made him one of the twenty wealthiest barons there. He had the whole of the Rape of Bramber (The word rape comes from the Old English word for rope, which was used to mark out territory). The Rape of Bramber was one of the six north-south sections into which

West Sussex was divided. Gillaume's name was anglicised as **William de Braose**, which was later spelled Breuse or Breos. Locals in Gower today pronounce it 'Bruce'.

His son **Philip** (died about 1150) became the first Lord of Builth and Radnor, the first de Braose holdings in Wales. There is evidence he went on the First Crusade, which was sent from Europe to try to regain the Holy Land lost to the Muslims. He became internationally recognised, referred to in a letter from the Archbishop of Canterbury to the pope as an example of piety. After his death, his son William II inherited lands in Sussex, Devon and Wales.

William II, the 3rd Lord of Bramber, married Bertha, daughter of Miles of Gloucester. She had four brothers who were expected to inherit, but they all died childless and the inheritance was split between the daughters. William and Bertha got Brecon and Abergavenny, which gave them a vast block of territory in the Middle March of Wales. William was close to King Stephen and also served King Henry II and was part of many of the king's expeditions in France. He was appointed sheriff of Hereford in 1173.

His son, **William III**, the 4th Lord of Bramber, inherited Bramber in Sussex, and Builth, Radnor, Brecknock and Abergavenny in the Welsh Marches, making him the strongest of the Marcher Barons. He fought beside King Richard many times, and held the office of Sheriff of Hereford for seven years. He supported King John against Arthur of Brittany in his claim to the throne. As a reward for supporting John over Arthur, William III became very influential and part of John's intimate circle. He and his wife Maud [or Mathilda] de St Valery had at least sixteen children.

King John, like his predecessors, had to keep a close watch over the vast Angevin empire. Learning that Hugh of Lusignan was planning to marry Isabella, heiress of the county of Angoulême, John feared it would give him too much territory. On 30 August 1200 John married her himself. Hugh immediately declared war, and other barons saw their own opportunities, including Arthur of Brittany.

In 1202, William de Braose was fighting along with John to rescue the dowager Queen Eleanor, who was being besieged at Mirabeau by Arthur of Brittany and his supporters. John's forces were victorious, and during the battle William captured Arthur. John imprisoned Arthur's supporters in Corfe Castle and starved them to death. Arthur himself was imprisoned at Rouen, guarded by William.

For some time there were rumours about Arthur's fate, but the truth was kept hidden. Later it emerged that on the night of 3 April 1203 John himself killed Arthur in a drunken rage and had his body tied to a stone and thrown in the River Seine. In February John gave William the Lordship of Gower in South Wales. Some think this was to reward him for the capture of Arthur, some for the more sinister motive of buying his silence over Arthur's death.

In addition to Gower, John gave William more land in Wales. He was also given custody of Glamorgan, Monmouth and Gwynllwg in return for large payments. John even made him Lord of Limerick in Ireland. His honours reached their peak when he was made Sheriff of Hereford in 1206. A full list of his lands is given at the end of the chapter.

William's influence at court however, lasted only a few years. Having used his lands as a buffer against the Welsh, John became concerned William was becoming too powerful, so John asked for money and some of William's sons as hostages to his loyalty. When William arrived home with the barons sent to collect his money and sons, William's wife Maud refused. A strong-willed woman, she said she would not hand over her sons to a murderer, who had assassinated his own nephew, Arthur. The barons and their men were shocked and went back and told John, and Maud speaking openly about John's secret sealed William's fate.

Later John would try to justify his actions. He wrote an open letter saying William had owed him a vast amount of money and had refused to hand over his lands as a forfeit for the debt. Kings raised money by taking payments for everything: inheritance rights, favourable judgements, marriage, even lands – John gave William many lands, but he was expected to pay for them all. As one of John's favourites, he probably didn't expect to actually pay all his debts. In fact John had already forgiven all the debts William owed to Henry II and Richard. It was a convenient way out for John, but it didn't explain the severity of his treatment.

John did call in a debt from William, and after a meeting, confiscated Brecon, Hay and Radnor and this time demanded William's grandsons as hostages. William agreed but immediately launched an unsuccessful rebellion with his sons **William IV** and **Reginald** in an attempt to recapture the castles. John dispossessed and outlawed William III in 1208. His wife Maud tried to placate John with a gift of Welsh white cattle, but to no avail.

The fall of William III left a vacuum in Wales, which was soon taken advantage of by Prince Gwenwynwyn of Powys and Prince Llywelyn of Gwynedd. William's sweep of land acted as a buffer between the Welsh and the Normans. Without William to keep the Welsh in check they quickly rebelled, and John was forced to launch a campaign to crush them.

William fled with his family to his estate in Ireland. This and other incidents persuaded John he should deal with the barons in Ireland: The Lacy brothers, Huw and Walter, were becoming powerful in Ireland; and when William Marshal, 1st Earl of Pembroke, angered John, he had fled to his Irish estate to wait for John to come round. So in 1210 John raised an army and a great fleet of ships, and in two months, conquered them all. John gave away the Lacy lands as punishment for sheltering William, and took William's lands for himself.

He didn't catch William though, who managed to escape to Wales where he was sheltered by Llywelyn ap Iorwerth, Prince of Gwynedd. This was surprising since Llywelyn was married to John's illegitimate daughter Joan. William later escaped to France through his port of Shoreham, disguised as a beggar. In France William told his secret about the death of Arthur of Brittany, which spread like wildfire, doing yet more damage to John's reputation. William's wife Maud and eldest son (William IV) were captured in Scotland, having been smuggled there from the north of Ireland. Many other family members were also rounded up.

William's wife and son were handed over to John, who locked them in a dungeon in Windsor Castle and left them to starve to death. A horror story is told that when the dungeon was opened, William IV was sat upright in a chair with his mother embracing him and apparently kissing his cheek. When they looked closer, they found his cheek had been chewed away. Two of William IV's children, John and Giles, were imprisoned at Corfe Castle in Dorset. Two others, Philip and Walter, were held at Angoulême in south-west France. They were not released until 1218, two years after King John's death.

Most of the barons were becoming increasingly unhappy with John's unpredictable behaviour and incompetent rule, but his treatment of William III and his family was the final straw. Many came out in open rebellion, which led eventually to Magna Carta, the Great Charter by which they hoped to bring John into line.

William III died a beggar in Paris in 1211. Stephen Langton, the Archbishop of Canterbury, who was also in Paris taking refuge from John, arranged for his burial in the Abbey of St Victoire. He had wanted to be buried in St John's, Brecon, but it was not to be.

The list of all William's lands is enormous (turn the page if this is boring):

Lands in Normandy:

Briouze; Walter de Lacy's lands; Longueil near Rouen and other strategic sites surrounding Norman centres.

Lands in England:

Bramber in Sussex; half barony of Barnstaple; Stratton St Margaret & Berewick in Wiltshire; King's Arley in Staffordshire; Tetbury & Hampnett in Gloucester; Walter de Lacy's lands in Gloucestershire, Herefordshire & Shropshire; John of Torrington's estates in Devon; half the barony of Totnes; Shoreham in Sussex; land in Warwickshire & Leicestershire; Buckingham Castle; Paddington & half the village of Gomshall in Surrey; Winton in Dorset; temporary custody of the lands of Gilbert of Monmouth; the wardship of Walter de Beauchamp with lands in Warwickshire & Berkshire.

Lands in Wales:

Radnor & surrounding land; Builth; Brecknock; Abergavenny; Elfael; Kington; Glamorgan; Gower; Grosmont, Skenfrith & Llantilio castles in Gwent.

Lands in Ireland:

County, city & region of Limerick; Carrickfergus castle in Ulster; lands in Tipperary; castle of Knocgrafan; William de Burgh's lands in Munster.

All are documented from original sources in Boulter, Matthew *The Career of William III de Briouze in the Reign of King John: Land, Power and Social Ties*

Chapter 4 – Suspicion and Coercion

Francis
08/13

King John used people. He had no concern for others except what he could get out of them. He didn't consider it his responsibility as king to serve the people, he considered that his position put a responsibility on others to serve him. What he wanted, he took, whether it was land, riches or someone else's wife.

In Europe at that time people believed in the divine right of kings: that God appointed the king to rule over them. The king was supposed to rule under God, with concern for God's commandments and God's love. John believed he had the right to have everything his own way, and would have huge tantrums when he was thwarted.

He seemed to have an insatiable sexual appetite, and would bed any woman he fancied, whether they be servant or nobility, wife or daughter of someone else, even of his loyal barons. He was known to actually demand of a baron to send his wife to John's bed.

Kings had always charged fees for allowing people their rightful inheritance, custody of land, judgements in law, wardship, advantageous marriages and so on, but John used to the full every method of making money, and made up a few of his own. Nicholas Stuteville was forced to pay 10,000 marks (approx. £3.6 million today) for his inheritance. William Mowbray, who had spent 4 years in Germany as a hostage for Richard's ransom, was charged 2,000 marks

17

(approx. £720,000 today) for John to hear a case regarding his barony, and then John found against him.

In 1204 King Philip of France captured Normandy. This was a bitter blow. All the noble families traced their lines back to Normandy. It had further repercussions too. Without lands abroad, the barons were much more concerned over their rights in their English lands and also sought to replace their French lands with conquests in Wales, Scotland and Ireland.

John was determined to regain the lost French lands but was thwarted again and again. In January 1205 he appointed constables to arrange training throughout the realm for all males over 12, and imposed fresh taxes to raise an army and sail to France in a huge fleet of ships. Most of the barons refused to support him and the project had to be abandoned. They claimed that since they now had no land in France, it had become foreign territory, and they had no obligation to fight in foreign wars.

During John's struggle with the pope he clamped down fiercely on his subjects, fearing they would turn against him. He demanded their children as hostages to their loyalty, and heaped outrages on them. He seized their castles and gave them to foreigners as bribes to serve in his army of mercenaries and found more and more ways to extort money from them. Coupled with his volatile temper and unstable mind, his barons felt less and less safe around him.

It was a vicious spiral. The more insecure John felt, the more cruel he was to his barons, which drove them away. Secret conspiracies were rife, and nobles in Wales, Ireland and Scotland all sought to take advantage of John's precarious position. As we have already seen, in 1211 John led an army to Ireland to deal with the rebellious barons there, especially Hugh de Lacy and William de Braose.

In 1212 Llywelyn ab Iorwerth, Prince of Gwynedd, conspired with Philip and the pope and launched a campaign in Wales. John's preparations to fight in France had to be postponed while he marched into Wales and had his fleet moved to Chester, but then he abandoned that campaign too. He was told of a conspiracy among his own followers. Egged on by the pope, Eustace de Vesci and Robert FitzWalter planned to assassinate the king or abandon him to his enemies in the forthcoming campaign. The King of Scotland too, was corresponding with the pope, whose excommunication of John made him fair game for all men faithful to the Church.

Amid all the mistakes, John could also be very astute. While all this was going on at home, he was forging alliances abroad that included his nephew the Emperor Otto IV of Germany, the Count of Flanders and the barons of Poitou in France. There were, however, two things that prevented John from making use of these alliances. He was not able to take his army abroad to fight for his French lands because of the rebellions at home, and his allies could not fight in support of an excommunicated king.

John had no concern for his soul, which is why the interdict and excommunication had no effect on him, but he had concern for his status and power, and that is why he eventually submitted to the pope. John agreed to accept Stephen Langton as Archbishop of Canterbury and all churchmen were ordered back to England to absolve John's sins. One of the bishops was Giles, son of William III de Braose. They arrived at Dover in 1213 and met John at Winchester. They had to obey the pope despite their hatred of John – they didn't believe his repentance for a minute.

In his submission he was totally shameless. When the exiled bishops returned, he grovelled at their feet. He gave his lands and crown to the papal legate, and vowed fealty as a vassal of the pope, agreeing to pay 1,000 marks (approx. £360,000 today) a year for his kingdom. It was not humiliating to John, though the rest of the court and the general populace were mortified and shocked, it was simply the means to an end, and it was a political triumph.

King Philip was planning to invade England and put his son Louis on the throne, and assembled a huge fleet of 1700 ships. On 28 May 1213 John's fleet of 500 ships fell on them in port and pillaged and burned them. With John repentant, this put a stop to Philip's plans, as there was no longer papal backing for an attack.

John's submission made little difference to his behaviour at home, and shortly afterwards an 'Unknown Charter of Liberties' was circulating. It is clear this was only a draft – some baron or clerk wishful thinking about concessions that could be wrung from the king, but it shows how the barons were already starting to think along those lines.

In February 1214 John began his French campaign. Otto's army, together with knights from Flanders and Boulogne, advanced from the Low Countries towards Paris, while John landed at La Rochelle, rallied his Poitevin barons, and struck northwards. All was going well until July, when John learned that Prince Louis and his army were coming to meet him. John retreated in disorder, claiming he was unable to face Louis because the Poitevin army failed to support him. That left Otto's forces to fight Philip alone. They met at Bouvines, where Otto was defeated. *[Some history books say that John's army fell apart at news of the defeat at Bouvines – the timeline is not clear]*

John France, professor emeritus in medieval history at Swansea University, called the Battle of Bouvines, '*the most important battle in English history that no-one has ever heard of.*' It was a turning-point in European history. Otto not only lost the battle, but his throne as well, and Philip became the most powerful monarch in Europe. It also marked the end of the Angevin empire. John now had no land in France.

John had believed that victory in France would not only remove the constant threat of Philip in France, but would also silence the barons and restore his prestige in England. Instead he returned to find the barons no longer hatching secret conspiracies, but openly discussing their demands. The orchestrator of these discussions was Archbishop Stephen Langton. He was determined to restore the old order of the realm. He met with the barons at Bury St Edmunds and introduced the idea of the old Charter issued by Henry I at his coronation. The idea was greeted with enthusiasm and the barons swore on the high altar that they would make John sign a similar Charter.

Chapter 5 - Magna Carta

At Christmas the barons came to John in arms and presented their claim. John stalled for time, promising an answer in the New Year, then on the feast of Epiphany (6 January 1215), then Easter. In the mean time John held individual interviews with each of the barons and tried to bribe, browbeat or persuade them over to his side, and asked them for a written promise not to demand such things of him or his successors again. Only three of them (the Earl of Chester, the Bishop of Winchester and William Brewer) joined him, the rest stood firm.

It was not just the barons who had had enough of John's behaviour. The clergy were angry over what they suffered during the interdict and the burghers of several towns felt that John had trampled on their ancient liberties. John sent commissioners to the County Courts to plead his case, but they returned with the news that no one would support him.

John then executed a master stroke against all his enemies: in March 1215 he took the Cross and pledged to go on Crusade. This put him even more under the protection of the pope, and any attack against him would be an affront to the pope himself. Had he actually gone on crusade, the barons' grievances would have had to wait until he returned, which may have been years. Who knows how history would have worked out then? However, it is likely that he had no intention of actually going.

His vow did not impress the barons, and when negotiations failed again in May, they renounced their obedience to him and went to war. The rebels included barons from most parts of the country, but since many of the major barons in the rebellion were from the Midlands or the North, chroniclers referred to them as the 'Northerners'. They first laid siege to Northampton Castle, but the garrison held out.

Then they received word from London that the townspeople would welcome them. The army marched to London led by Robert FitzWalter, calling himself 'The Marshal of the Army of God and the Holy Church.' The rebels could do piety too. London, where the king had his capital and administrative centre, opened her gates to them. The example was followed by Exeter and Lincoln, and promises of aid came from Scotland and Wales.

John had written letters to the pope, but it took a month to reach Rome, so they were too late. He had summoned mercenaries from abroad, but they too took time to arrive. He was left with no choice – he had to talk to the barons about their demands. The rebels were in London, the king was at Windsor, so they met half way, in a meadow near Staines, called Runnymede.

All the major players were there. Archbishop Stephen Langton, Pandulf the papal legate, and all the senior bishops represented the church. William Marshal, Hubert de Burgh, the earls of Salisbury, Warren and Arundel and a host of other dignitaries and warriors represented both sides.

A preliminary draft known as 'The Articles of the Barons' was discussed, and a final version agreed and sealed by John on 15 June. This was the nearest England has ever come to a written constitution. When the rest of the rebel barons examined the agreement, not all were satisfied, and some rode away, but most of them were persuaded after a few days.

On 19 June the barons renewed their homage to the king and peace was proclaimed. Multiple copies were hurriedly made and issued to cathedrals and other significant places around the country, to make sure the news spread far and wide that John had made this agreement.

The charter began life as a peace agreement between a king and his people, a way to end the threat of civil war. The rebels however were well aware that a list of their demands for reparation would reflect badly on themselves. Holding a king to ransom under threat of war is just bullying and selfishness. They needed to be able to justify their actions.

And so the charter evolved into something with wider concerns, that could be promoted as seeking justice in a wide range of areas. They ended up by demanding a charter that was long, detailed and contained something for everyone. It became not just a criticism of the way John had been treating his barons, but a commentary on a whole system of government.

Chapter 6 - What did Magna Carta say?

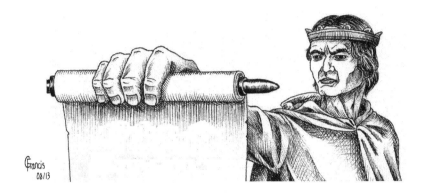

Francis
08/13

The Magna Carta was not the first charter by a king of England for the people. In fact, it was based on 'the laws of the Confessor' and the charter of Henry I.

Edward the Confessor (1041-1065) was a weak king but he was very pious and beloved by his people. His reign became legendary in contrast to the brutality of the Norman kings. His laws weren't written down until long after his death. They all related to peace – defining the peace of the church and the peace of the king, and the enforcement of the peace.

Although he was a son of William the Conqueror, when Henry I was crowned he wanted to make it clear that he was not like the kings who went before – his father William and his brother William Rufus. He issued a charter on 5 August 1100, which was widely circulated, confirming the laws of the Confessor and amending the unfair laws enforced by the two Williams.

Magna Carta was very similar, in that it sought to restate the laws King John had flouted and abused, but in order to prevent future misuse, it spelled out the rights of the people in exact detail. Some rights were in common acceptance but had never been written down, others were open to abuse and were clarified, and yet others went further into new territory where it was felt they needed protection from the king.

The contents fall into four basic headings: purely baronial

grievances, wider issues touching on the law, clauses benefiting the rebels' allies, and those aspects which really do bear upon the common good and 'liberty' as it would be understood today.

The charter contains 63 clauses, which are not numbered or in any particular order. The text just runs on from one item to the next. We number them today for ease of reference. Because the parchment it was written on was very expensive, the Latin writing was very small, and some words were abbreviated, making it very hard to read. While they were seeking to remedy King John's behaviour, the barons and churchmen also strove to be scrupulously fair, so that he would have no excuse for refusing it. A full translation is in the Appendix.

The charter begins by giving King John his full title: '*by the grace of God King of England, Lord of Ireland, Duke of Normandy and Aquitaine, and Count of Anjou*', despite the fact that the French lands had been lost. Then it lists all those present. This included representatives of the Church and the barons, especially Stephen Langton, the Archbishop of Canterbury, and William Marshal, Earl of Pembroke (a very significant figure in history).

This is a summary of the topics covered:

- The rights of the Church and cities (still in force today).

- Rules on inheritance, with special mention of under-age heirs and widows.

- Handling of debts, rent, service due and various obligations.

- Restrictions on raising aid by the king from the country and by a baron from his lands.

- Goods, corn, horses, carts and wood are not to be taken without payment.

- Rules for the treatment of foreign merchants and those who return from abroad.

- A large group of clauses concerned justice: Establishing free and fair justice for all (still in force today), and rules about when and where courts were to be held, by whom, and restricting punishments. No fine could be levied which would deprive a man of his livelihood, for example.

- The other large group of clauses concerned redress for a long list of King John's abuses.

The charter finished by urging all men to treat each other in the same way as laid out for King John, and a long section setting up a supervisory group of 25 barons to see that the king kept to the charter. These 25 barons had the power to seize the king's property or take other measures if he failed to keep the terms agreed. They clearly didn't trust John at all, and they were right.

Paradoxically, it was this very provision which was the charter's undoing. No king can be expected to voluntarily agree to clauses which effectively put 25 men ahead of the king. When John first saw the clauses he flew into a rage, crying, *'They have given me five-and-twenty over-kings.'* Of course, when the committee of 25 was chosen, they were all John's enemies. It was impossible to expect John to tolerate such conditions.

Contrary to many illustrations, King John didn't sign the charter, in fact he probably couldn't write (he had men to do that for him). Instead He fixed his official seal to it. It was immediately copied (complete with spelling mistakes) up to 13 times and sent to important places around the country, including the great cathedrals. They wanted to be certain everyone would know what it contained and that John had agreed. In the words of one historian, *'Magna Carta had gone viral.'*

Only four copies of the charter now remain. Two are kept in the British Library, one in Salisbury and one in Lincoln.

The clauses clearly demonstrate the abuses that John had perpetrated against his subjects. Rules on inheritance, because John would confiscate estates on the pretext of looking after under-age heirs. Rules about widows, whose marriage John had been known to sell to the highest bidder. Rules to prevent John raising rents and other fees whenever he liked.

The most important clause today is the one on justice, which is still in force, and enshrined in every civilised country's laws:

(39) No freeman shall be seized or imprisoned, or stripped of his rights or possessions, or outlawed or exiled, or deprived of his standing in any other way, nor will we proceed with force against him, or send others to do so, except by the lawful judgement of his equals or by the law of the land.

To modern minds this basic right is obvious, but in medieval times up to this point a person could be punished at the whim of his lord, and anyone, lords included, could be punished by the king. Not just punished either. Your lord could take away your goods, your land, or your children and give no reason. Magna Carta marks the first time the king was made to be subject to the law rather than above it.

However, the clauses in the charter only spelled out the rights of *free men*. Clause 1 states that the liberties were confirmed '*to all freemen of my kingdom and their heirs for ever.*' The majority of the population were not free, they were *villeins*, regarded as the property of the lord who owned the land on which they lived or worked. They were only protected as part of the lords' valuable property.

Those who were considered *free men* fell into four categories:

The aristocracy (lords, barons, earls etc.): Their rights come first because it was these men who brought King John to the situation where he had no choice but to agree the charter.

The church: The main force behind Magna Carta was the Archbishop of Canterbury Stephen Langton. While it was the barons who had the greatest grievances against John, with his treatment of William de Braose and his family the prime example, the Archbishop was a learned man and helped frame the document. He made sure that the church benefited as well.

Tenants and minor lords: The show of force by the barons consisted of the men they could muster to fight. They secured the support of their men by ensuring there were provisions in the charter for them too. Clauses 15 and 60 stated that the rights which were granted by the king to the barons would also be granted by the barons to their own vassals.

Merchants and traders: The charter confirms existing customs and privileges, which they had already won for themselves, so although they are mentioned, they actually received very little that was new.

The Confessor's Law and Henry's Charter had made general statements, assuming that men would know what was meant and be reasonable and fair in their interpretation. John's behaviour had shown that the law needed to be explicitly stated, and the king made to obey. The divine right of kings was over. From now on, the king would be as subject to the law as everyone else.

Chapter 7 Civil War

Francis
08/13

For those of us who know little of history, Magna Carta is held up as a great blow for democracy, and we may think once John sealed it, it was all over. The truth is very different. As a document guaranteeing the freedoms of John's subjects, it failed, because John simply ignored it.

While the negotiations were going on, John had written to the pope. With no knowledge of Magna Carta, on 18 June the pope wrote a letter to the barons threatening them with excommunication if they did not come to terms with John. On 7 July he wrote to Pandulf his legate and some other senior churchmen giving them authority to excommunicate anyone who opposed John and interfered with his crusade. He also suspended Stephen Langton.

When the pope heard about Magna Carta, he promptly annulled it. '*Under threat of excommunication we order that the king should not dare to observe and the barons and their associates should not insist on it being observed. The charter with all its undertakings and guarantees we declare to be null and void of all validity for ever*' he wrote. On 5 September the churchmen excommunicated the rebel barons.

Frustrated, the barons went to war again, but this time went one step further. The problem with their rebellion, was that previous rebellions had been in support of a rival candidate, but they had no alternative candidate for the throne. King Philip of France's son Louis was married to the granddaughter of Henry II, so they invited him to take the throne of England, believing this would bring a French army to their aid. They also gave lands along the Scottish border to Alexander II, King of Scotland, to ensure his support for their cause.

John, with his loyal barons and an army of mercenaries, treated the rebels and their lands like a hostile country. He worked his way through the Midlands and the North like a scourge: raping, killing, looting and burning. The only escape was to pay protection money. At night he would send out his men to burn and uproot everything within a ten-mile radius.

The Yorkshire rebels took refuge with King Alexander. In January 1216 saying, '*by God's teeth, we will run the little sandy fox cub to his earth*', John marched into the Scottish lowlands, the first invasion of Scotland since 1072. He only stayed 10 days, but he made his mark on several towns and burned Berwick to the ground after torturing the townspeople.

John worked his way back south, destroying the countryside, towns and villages as he went, heading for London, where the rebels were based, pinned down by the forces he had left behind. The rebels began to lose heart, and the trickle of those who came to make peace with John was soon turning into a flood. Victory was in his grasp. On 17 April he announced one last chance, calling on all rebels to submit by 24 May or forfeit their lands.

He gave orders to gather his ships in the Thames estuary to prevent a French landing, and marched his army to Dover. On the evening of 18 May John's luck changed again. A tremendous storm came down The English Channel and smashed his ships at their moorings. Two days later, as the weather calmed, Louis sailed his army past them and landed at Thanet.

Most of John's mercenaries were French, and they refused to fight against their Prince, so Louis was unopposed by land or sea, and won that fight without a blow being struck. Louis marched into London on 2 June, to an uproarious welcome. The rebel barons knelt and paid him homage. Alexander II even marched all the way from Scotland to pay homage to Louis.

The pope imposed an interdict on London, but the burghers ignored it, saying he had no authority over secular matters, and mass continued to be celebrated. Four days later Louis headed out of London again in pursuit of John.

But once again fate favoured John. Louis, it turned out, was hopeless at seigecraft. Not one of the royal castles fell, except where Louis eventually managed to starve them out. In addition, the old rivalries between the French and the English were erupting all over the army. In London, the French soldiers had taken full advantage of the taverns and the brothels and generally made nuisances of themselves. In the field, the hated French were deserting every day.

John had retreated to the Welsh Marches to try to gain the support of Llywelyn ab Iorwerth and the Marcher barons, without success. Now he marched east, hoping to catch Alexander on his way home to Scotland. There were rumours that Alexander's forces were joining Gilbert de Gant's army at Lincoln, but when John reached Lincoln in September, they had already gone northwards.

In October there was a skirmish at Lynn (now called Kings Lynn). John fell ill with dysentery, and, refusing to rest, he pressed on towards Wisbech. The exact details of what happened next, historians have failed to discover, but the loss of John's baggage in The Wash is a story that has passed into legend.

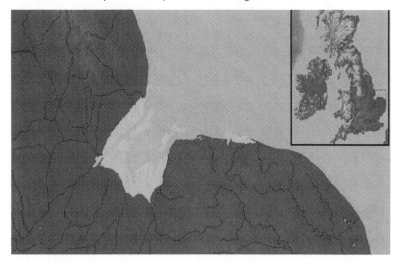

31

The Wash is the large indentation in the coastline of eastern England that separates the curved coast of East Anglia from Lincolnshire [see map]. Owing to deposits of sediment, the coastline has dramatically altered over time, and in places the water is very shallow, with sandbanks and quicksands. Apparently John's baggage train, or part of it, attempted to cross the mouth of the River Wellstream before the tide had fully receded, and much of it became trapped and sank in the quicksands. John lost a lot, but most importantly, he lost the crown jewels.

On the evening of 12 October John reached Swineshead and was struck down with grief and rage at the news. He unwisely tucked into a dish of peaches in new cider, which did him no good, considering his dysentery. On 14 October he was so ill he could barely sit in the saddle, but he insisted on pressing on. He eventually admitted defeat and his men fashioned a crude litter to carry him, which actually made his suffering worse.

He eventually made it to Newark where he collapsed and may have had at least one heart attack. The Abbot of Croxton heard his confession and gave him the last sacraments. He named his son Henry as his heir and William Marshal as regent and guardian of his two sons, and made a short will. He also asked to be buried in the Church of the Blessed Virgin and St Wulfstan in Worcester. Shortly after midnight, in the early hours of 19 October 1216, John died.

John's household did not grieve for him. They made off with as much loot as they could carry away before the officials came for the body. It was dressed in finery, escorted to Worcester by mercenaries in full armour, and laid in St Wulfstan's chapel.

Chapter 8 - King Henry III & Magna Carta

King John   King Henry III

William Marshal was one of the greatest men in English history. He had already served Henry II, the Young King Henry, Richard and John. When he was asked to become regent and guardian of John's two sons, he was nearly 70 years old, at a time when you were considered old at 40. Once again he stepped up to the mark.

Henry III was crowned hurriedly at Gloucester, away from Louis and his forces. Henry's advisers, especially William Marshal, were well-respected men who would see to it that John's abuses would not be continued. To that end, within a month Henry's advisers re-issued Magna Carta without it's more objectionable clauses and vowed to see it kept. Depriving a child of his inheritance was disapproved of, and the people would much rather have an English king than one from the hated French. All these factors removed the need for civil war.

Louis was the one who lost out. His supporters streamed away and paid homage to the new king. He was forced to rely more and more on his French soldiers, which only increased his unpopularity. William Marshal was determined to remove Louis and his forces from England, and led the campaign himself. On 20 May 1217 the Earl Marshal led the attack, against a joint army of English and French, to relieve the siege of Lincoln Castle and won a decisive victory.

In September, a second French fleet carrying reinforcements was defeated, and Louis entered into peace talks. The Treaty of Lambeth was signed, in which Louis recognised Henry as king of England, acknowledged his right to the Channel Islands, promised to help him recover his father's continental possessions and agreed never to aid Henry's rebellious subjects. Prisoners on both sides were released and the rebel barons restored to their lands. In return William Marshal secretly paid him £7,000. Some barons objected to buying him off and wanted to continue the fight, but William Marshal wanted a quick end to the conflict.

It is at this point that Magna Carta got it's name. One of the major abuses by John was in the area of the Forest Laws. A whole different set of rules applied to anywhere designated as a forest, including the cutting of wood that was essential to daily life. One of the things the charter imposed on John was to 'deforest' large areas of land. This did not mean to destroy the forests, merely to take them out of the Forest Law. A separate charter was issued under Henry III which only related to Forest Law. This was much shorter, so the main charter became known as the 'big charter' – Magna Carta.

William Marshal died in May 1219 after a long life in service of his country. Henry went on to become one of the longest-reigning monarchs, reigning 56 years (1216-72), only superseded 600 years later by George III (1760-1820). Unfortunately he did not prove to be a good king. The treasury was bankrupt, so he had to rely on unpopular taxes, and he proved to be insensitive and incompetent. In the latter years of his reign the country once again plunged into civil war, only this time it was rescued by his eldest son, Edward, who took over the reins until Henry died and then became King Edward I.

In 1225 the charter was reissued yet again, and this version is particularly important. This is the version, and not the Runnymede charter, that entered the statute books. This is the version that has influenced government ever since. Like the charter of 1215, these reissues were translated into French and English and read out at meetings of the Shire courts throughout the realm. All this meant that Magna Carta was a highly publicised concept.

When lawyers compiled the books of statutes it was always Magna Carta, the text of 1225 as confirmed in 1297, that had pride of place. It came to be thought of as the first statute of the realm.

Conclusion

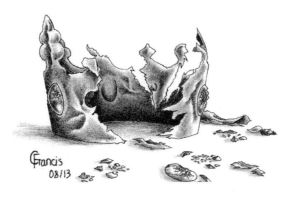

Francis
08/13

King John's unpredictable and violent behaviour alienated the barons. He was not concerned with right and wrong, but saw justice as a tool for favouring his friends and attacking his enemies, and for raising revenue. The barons felt he tampered with justice in order to persecute them and trample on their rights. His treatment of William III de Braose and his wife and son was the final straw that led to their rebellion.

Magna Carta was simply an attempt at a peace treaty between a recalcitrant king and his exasperated people. Many of its clauses dealt with specific things King John had done, and were dropped in later versions. Many of its clauses are not even understood today and need a good deal of background explanation. And it was only in force for about ten weeks.

It should have slipped away into forgotten history, but for its central, revolutionary ideas: that even the king is not above the law, and justice is the right of every man. This idea, once expressed, could not be un-thought. Subsequent kings latched on to it as a kind of election manifesto, a way of winning the confidence of the people. The people in their turn latched on to it as a definition of the way kings should behave. Whenever a king started to misrule, the cry went up for the charter.

In 1265 when the government of England was in the hands of Simon de Montfort it was decreed that the charter should be proclaimed twice a year so that in future no one could claim to be ignorant of it. Edward I was forced to confirm the charter in 1297. In the 17th century, a series of kings – James I, Charles I and James II – tried to assert the divine right of kings, and were challenged in the courts and by Parliament, using Magna Carta.

The charter originally set out to define the liberties of the people, but it came to be more of a symbol that people should have liberty, as future generations interpreted the clauses in their own way. Starting in 1829, various sections were repealed: some had become outdated, some superseded by other statutes. But four remain in force today. Two concern the freedom of the city of London and the Church, but it is the other two that carry the most weight for the most people.

No freeman shall be seized or imprisoned, or stripped of his rights or possessions, or outlawed or exiled, or deprived of his standing in any other way, nor will we proceed with force against him, or send others to do so, except by the lawful judgement of his equals or by the law of the land. (Clause 39)

To no one will we sell, to no one deny or delay right or justice. (Clause 40)

It is these clauses that underpin not only the UK's constitutional framework, but that of many other countries, including the USA. The Pilgrim Fathers took the ideas with them and American law says today, *No person shall be deprived of life, liberty or property without due process of law.* As the British Empire spread around the globe, they also spread the ideas in Magna Carta. Originally intended for only Freemen, over the centuries all men, all people, have been declared free and entitled to the same justice.

If you enjoyed this book, please leave a review on Amazon and help spread the word! Thank you.

Bibliography

Boulter, Matthew *The Career of William III de Briouze in the Reign of King John: Land, Power and Social Ties*

Danziger, Danny & Gillingham, John *1215 The Year of Magna Carta*

Ericson, Carolly, *Brief Lives of the English Monarchs*

Green, J R *A Short History Of The English People,* volume 1

King, Edmund *Medieval England: From Hastings to Bosworth*

McLynn, Frank *Lionheart and Lackland: King Richard, King John and the Wars of Conquest*

Thomas, Ann Marie *Broken Reed: The Lords of Gower and King John*

Turner, Ralph V. *King John: England's Evil King?*

Wilson, Derek *The Plantagenets: The Kings That Made Britain*

Online sources:

BBC News Magazine *The most important battle you've probably never heard of*
http://www.bbc.co.uk/news/magazine-28484146

British Library website
http://www.bl.uk/treasures/magnacarta/index.html

Index on Censorship *The Magna Carta Legacy*
http://www.indexoncensorship.org/2014/12/john-crace-1215/

ITV News website *PM calls for British values push: What you need to know about Magna Carta* http://www.itv.com/news/2014-06-15/pm-calls-for-british-values-push-what-you-need-to-know-about-magna-carta/

Magna Carta 800th *The History of Magna Carta*
http://magnacarta800th.com/history-of-the-magna-carta/

Online Library of Liberty *Magna Carta: A Commentary on the Great Charter of King John, with an Historical Introduction [1215]*
http://oll.libertyfund.org/titles/338

The Guardian newspaper website *Magna Carta 800 years on: recognition at last for 'England's greatest export'*
http://www.theguardian.com/culture/2014/nov/01/magna-carta-800-celebrates-anniversary

Appendix

Translation of Magna Carta from the British Library website
http://www.bl.uk/treasures/magnacarta/index.html

JOHN, by the grace of God King of England, Lord of Ireland, Duke of Normandy and Aquitaine, and Count of Anjou, to his archbishops, bishops, abbots, earls, barons, justices, foresters, sheriffs, stewards, servants, and to all his officials and loyal subjects, greeting.

Know that before God, for the health of our soul and those of our ancestors and heirs, to the honour of God, the exhortation of the holy Church, and the better ordering of our kingdom, at the advice of our reverend fathers Stephen, archbishop of Canterbury, primate of all England, and cardinal of the holy Roman Church, Henry archbishop of Dublin, William bishop of London, Peter bishop of Winchester, Jocelyn bishop of Bath and Glastonbury, Hugh bishop of Lincoln, Walter bishop of Worcester, William bishop of Coventry, Benedict bishop of Rochester, Master Pandulf subdeacon and member of the papal household, Brother Aymeric master of the knighthood of the Temple in England, William Marshal earl of Pembroke, William earl of Salisbury, William earl of Warren, William earl of Arundel, Alan de Galloway constable of Scotland, Warin Fitz Gerald, Peter Fitz Herbert, Hubert de Burgh seneschal of Poitou, Hugh de Neville, Matthew Fitz Herbert, Thomas Basset, Alan Basset, Philip Daubeny, Robert de Roppeley, John Marshall, John Fitz Hugh, and other loyal subjects:

(1) FIRST, THAT WE HAVE GRANTED TO GOD, and by this present charter have confirmed for us and our heirs in perpetuity, that the English Church shall be free, and shall have its rights undiminished, and its liberties unimpaired. That we wish this so to be observed, appears from the fact that of our own free will, before the outbreak of the present dispute between us and our barons, we granted and confirmed by charter the freedom of the Church's elections – a right reckoned to be of the greatest necessity and importance to it – and caused this to be confirmed by Pope Innocent III. This freedom we shall observe ourselves, and desire to be observed in good faith by our heirs in perpetuity.

TO ALL FREE MEN OF OUR KINGDOM we have also granted, for us and our heirs for ever, all the liberties written out below, to have and to keep for them and their heirs, of us and our heirs:

(2) If any earl, baron, or other person that holds lands directly of the Crown, for military service, shall die, and at his death his heir shall be of full age and owe a 'relief', the heir shall have his inheritance on payment of the ancient scale of 'relief'. That is to say, the heir or heirs of an earl shall pay £100 for the entire earl's barony, the heir or heirs of a knight 100s at most for the entire knight's 'fee', and any man that holds less shall pay less in accordance with the ancient usage of 'fees'.

(3) But if the heir of such a person is under age and a ward, when he comes of age he shall have his inheritance without 'relief' or fine.

(4) The guardian of the land of any heir who is under age shall take from it only reasonable revenues, customary dues, and feudal services. He shall do this without destruction or damage to men or property. If we have given the guardianship of the land to a sheriff, or to any person answerable to us for the revenues, and he commits destruction or damage, we will exact compensation from him, and the land shall be entrusted to two worthy and prudent men of the same 'fee', who shall be answerable to us for the revenues, or to the person to whom we have assigned them. If we have given or sold to anyone the guardianship of such land, and he causes destruction or damage, he shall lose the guardianship of it, and it shall be handed over to two worthy and prudent men of the same 'fee', who shall be similarly answerable to us.

(5) For so long as the Guardian has guardianship of such land, he shall maintain the houses, parks, fish preserves, ponds, mills, and everything else pertaining to it, from the revenues of the land itself. When the heir comes of age, he shall restore the whole land to him, stocked with plough teams and such implements of husbandry as the season demands and the revenues from the land can reasonably bear.

(6) Heirs may be given in marriage, but not to someone of lower social standing. Before a marriage takes place, it shall be made known to the heir's next-of-kin.

(7) At her husband's death, a widow may have her marriage portion

and inheritance at once and without trouble. She shall pay nothing for her dower, marriage portion, or any inheritance that she and her husband held jointly on the day of his death. She may remain in her husband's house for forty days after his death, and within this period her dower shall be assigned to her.

(8) No widow shall be compelled to marry, so long as she wishes to remain without a husband. But she must give security that she will not marry without royal consent, if she holds her land of the Crown, or without the consent of whatever other lord she may hold them of.

(9) Neither we nor our officials will seize any land or rent in payment of a debt, so long as the debtor has movable goods sufficient to discharge the debt. A debtor's sureties shall not be distrained upon so long as the debtor himself can discharge his debt. If, for lack of means, the debtor is unable to discharge his debt, his sureties shall be answerable for it. If they so desire, they may have the debtor's lands and rents until they have received satisfaction for the debt that they paid for him, unless the debtor can show that he had settled his obligations to them.

(10) If anyone who has borrowed a sum of money from Jews dies before the debt has been repaid, his heirs shall pay no interest on the debt for so long as he remains under age, irrespective of whom he holds his land. If such a debt falls into the hands of the Crown, it will take nothing except the principal sum specified in the bond.

(11) If a man dies owing money to Jews, his wife may have her dower and pay nothing towards the debt from it. If he leaves children that are under age, their needs may also be provided for on a scale appropriate to the size of his holding of land. The debt is to be paid out of the residue, reserving the service due to his feudal lords. Debts owed to persons other than Jews are to be dealt with similarly.

(12) No 'scutage' or 'aid' may be levied in our kingdom without its general consent, unless it is for the ransom of our person, to make our eldest son a knight, and (once) to marry our eldest daughter. For these purposes only reasonable 'aid' may be levied. 'Aids' from the city of London are to be treated similarly.

(13) The city of London shall enjoy all its ancient liberties and free

customs, both by land and by water. We also will and grant that all other cities, boroughs, towns, and ports shall enjoy all their liberties and free customs.

(14) To obtain the general consent of the realm for the assessment of an 'aid' – except in the three cases specified above – or a 'scutage', we will cause the archbishops, bishops, abbots, earls, and greater barons to be summoned individually by letter. To those who hold lands directly of us we will cause a general summons to be issued, through the sheriffs and other officials, to come together on a fixed day (of which at least forty days notice shall be given) and at a fixed place. In all letters of summons, the cause of the summons will be stated. When a summons has been issued, the business appointed for the day shall go forward in accordance with the resolution of those present, even if not all those who were summoned have appeared.

(15) In future we will allow no one to levy an 'aid' from his free men, except to ransom his person, to make his eldest son a knight, and (once) to marry his oldest daughter. For these purposes only a reasonable 'aid' may be levied.

(16) No man shall be forced to perform more service for a knight's 'fee', or any other free holding of land, than is due from it.

(17) Ordinarily lawsuits shall not follow the royal court around, but shall be held in a fixed place.

(18) Inquests of *novel disseisin, mort d'ancestor,* and *darrein presentment* shall be taken only in their proper county court. We ourselves, or in our absence abroad our chief justice, will send two justices to each county four times a year, and these justices, with four knights of the county elected by the county itself, shall hold the assizes in the county court, on the day and in the place where the court meets.

(19) If any assizes cannot be taken on the day of the county court, as many knights and freeholders shall afterwards remain behind, of those who have attended the court, as will suffice for the administration of justice, having regard to the volume of business to be done.

(20) For a trivial offence, a free man shall be fined only in proportion to the degree of his offence, and for a serious offence correspondingly, but not so heavily as to deprive him of his livelihood. In the same way, a merchant shall be spared his merchandise, and a villein the implements of his husbandry, if they fall upon the mercy of a royal court. None of these fines shall be imposed except by the assessment on oath of reputable men of the neighbourhood.

(21) Earls and barons shall be fined only by their equals, and in proportion to the gravity of their offence.

(22) A fine imposed upon the late property of a clerk in holy orders shall be assessed upon the same principles, without reference to the value of his ecclesiastical benefice.

(23) No town or person shall be forced to build bridges over rivers except those with an ancient obligation to do so.

(24) No sheriff, constable, coroners, or other royal officials are to hold lawsuits that should be held by the royal justices.

(25) Every county, hundred, wappentake, and riding shall remain at its ancient rent, without increase, except the royal demesne manors.

(26) If at the death of a man who holds a lay 'fee' of the Crown, a sheriff or royal official produces royal letters patent of summons for a debt due to the Crown, it shall be lawful for them to seize and list movable goods found in the lay 'fee' of the dead man to the value of the debt, as assessed by worthy men. Nothing shall be removed until the whole debt is paid, when the residue shall be given over to the executors to carry out the dead man's will. If no debt is due to the Crown, all the movable goods shall be regarded as the property of the dead man, except the reasonable shares of his wife and children.

(27) If a free man dies intestate, his movable goods are to be distributed by his next-of-kin and friends, under the supervision of the church. The rights of his debtors are to be preserved.

(28) No constable or other royal official shall take corn or other movable goods from any man without immediate payment, unless the seller voluntarily offers postponement of this.

(29) No constable may compel a knight to pay money for castle-guard

if the knight is willing to undertake the guard in person, or with reasonable excuse to supply some other fit man to do it. A knight taken or sent on military service shall be excused from castle-guard for the period of this service.

(30) No sheriff, royal official, or other person shall take horses or carts for transport from any freeman, without his consent.

(31) Neither we nor any royal official will take wood for our castle, or for any other purpose, without the consent of the owner.

(32) We will not keep the lands of people convicted of felony in our hand for longer than a year and a day, after which they shall be returned to the lords of the 'fees' concerned.

(33) All fish-weirs shall be removed from the Thames, the Medway, and throughout the whole of England, except on the sea coast.

(34) The writ called *precipe* shall not in future be issued to anyone in respect of any holding of land, if a free man could thereby be deprived of the right of trial in his own Lord's court.

(35) There shall be standard measures of wine, ale, and corn (the London quarter), throughout the kingdom. There shall also be a standard width of dyed cloth, russet, and haberject, namely two ells within the selvedges. Weights are to be standardised similarly.

(36) In future nothing shall be paid or accepted for the issue of a writ of inquisition of life or limbs. It shall be given gratis, and not refused.

(37) If a man hold land of the Crown by 'fee-farm', 'socage', or 'burgage', and also holds land of someone else for knight's service, we will not have guardianship of his heir, nor of the land that belongs to the other person's fee, by virtue of the 'fee-farm', 'socage', or 'burgage', unless the 'fee-farm' owes knight's service. We will not have the guardianship of a man's heir, or of land that he holds of someone else, by reason of any small property that he may hold of the Crown for a service of knives, arrows, or the like.

(38) In future no official shall place a man on trial upon his own unsupported statement, without producing credible witnesses to the truth of it.

(39) No freeman shall be seized or imprisoned, or stripped of his rights or possessions, or outlawed or exiled, or deprived of his standing in any other way, nor will we proceed with force against him, or send others to do so, except by the lawful judgement of his equals or by the law of the land.

(40) To no one will we sell, to no one deny or delay right or justice.

(41) All merchants may enter or leave England unharmed and without fear, and may stay or travel within it, by land or water, for purposes of trade, free from all illegal exactions, in accordance with ancient and lawful customs. This, however, does not apply in time of war to merchants from a country that is at war with us. Any such merchants found in our country at the outbreak of war shall be detained without injury to their persons or property, until we or our chief justice have discovered how our own merchants are being treated in the country at war with us. If our own merchants are safe they should be safe too.

(42) In future it shall be lawful for any man to leave and return to our kingdom unharmed and without fear, by land or water, preserving his allegiance to us, except in time of war, for some short period, for the common benefit of the realm. People that have been imprisoned or outlawed in accordance with the law of the land, people from a country that is at war with us, and merchants – who shall be dealt with as stated above – are excepted from this provision.

(43) If a man holds lands of any 'escheat' such as the 'honour' of Wallingford, Nottingham, Boulogne, Lancaster, or of other 'escheats' in our hand that are baronies, at his death his heir shall give us only the 'relief' and service that he would have made to the baron, had the barony been in the baron's hand. We will hold the 'escheat' in the same manner as the baron held it.

(44) People who live outside the forest need not in future appear before the royal justices of the forest in answer to general summonses, unless they are actually involved in proceedings or are sureties for someone who has been seized for forest offence.

(45) We will appoint as justices, constables, sheriffs, or other officials, only men that know the law of the realm and are minded to keep it

well.

(46) All barons who have founded abbeys, and have charters of English kings or ancient tenure as evidence of this, may have guardianship of them when there is no abbot, as is their due.

(47) All forests that have been created in our reign shall at once be disafforested. River-banks that have been in closed in our reign shall be treated similarly.

(48) All evil customs relating to forests and warrens, foresters, warreners, sheriffs and their servants, or river-banks and their wardens, are at once to be investigated in every county by twelve sworn knights of the county, and within forty days of their enquiry the evil customs are to be abolished completely and irrevocably. But we, or our chief justice if we are not in England, are first to be informed.

(49) We will at once return all hostages and charters delivered up to us by Englishmen as security for peace or for loyal service.

(50) We will remove completely from their offices the kinsman of Gerard de Athée, and in future they shall hold no offices in England. The people in question are Engelard de Cigogné, Peter, Guy, and Andrew de Chanceaux, Guy de Cigogné, Geoffrey de Martigny and his brothers, Philip Marc and his brothers, with Geoffrey his nephew, and all their followers.

(51) As soon as peace is restored, we will remove from the kingdom all the foreign knights, bowman, their attendants, and the mercenaries that have come to it, to its harm, with horses and arms.

(52) To any man who we have deprived or dispossessed of land, castles, liberties, or rights, without the lawful judgement of his equals, we will at once restore these. In cases of dispute the matter shall be resolved by the judgement of the twenty-five barons referred to below in the clause for securing the peace. In cases, however, where a man was deprived or dispossessed of something without the lawful judgement of his equals by our father King Henry or our brother King Richard, and it remains in our hands or is held by others under our warranty, we shall have respite for the period commonly allowed to Crusaders, unless a lawsuit has been begun, or an enquiry

had been made at our order, before we took the Cross as a Crusader. On our return from the Crusade, or if we abandon it, we will at once render justice in full.

(53) We shall have similar respite in rendering justice in connection with forests that are to be disafforested, or to remain forests, when these were first afforested by our father Henry or our brother Richard; with the guardianship of lands in another person's 'fee', where we have hitherto had this by virtue of a 'fee' held of us for knight's service by a third party; and with abbeys founded in another person's 'fee', in which the lord of the 'fee' claims to own a right. On our return from the Crusade or if we abandon it, we will at once do full justice to complaints about these matters.

(54) No one shall be arrested or imprisoned on the appeal of a woman for the death of any person except her husband.

(55) All fines that have been given to us unjustly and against the law of the land, and all fines that we have exacted unjustly, shall be entirely remitted or the matter decided by a majority judgement of the twenty-five barons referred to below in the clause for securing the peace together with Stephen, archbishop of Canterbury, if he can be present, and such others as he wishes to bring with him. If the archbishop cannot be present, proceedings shall continue without him, provided that if any of the twenty-five barons has been involved in a similar suit himself, his judgement shall be set aside, and someone else chosen and sworn in his place, as a substitute for the single occasion, by the rest of the twenty-five.

(56) If we have deprived or dispossessed any Welshman of lands, liberties or anything else in England or in Wales, without the lawful judgement of their equals, these are at once to be returned to them. A dispute on this point shall be determined in the Marches by the judgement of equals. English law shall apply to holdings of land in England, Welsh law to those in Wales, and the law of the Marches to those in the Marches. The Welsh shall treat us and ours in the same way.

(57) In cases where a Welshman was deprived or dispossessed of anything, without the lawful judgement of his equals, by our father King Henry or our brother King Richard, and it remains in our hands

or is held by others under our warranty, we shall have respite for the period commonly allowed to Crusaders, unless the lawsuit had been begun or an enquiry had been made at our order, before we took the Cross as a Crusader. But on our return from the Crusade, or if we abandon it, we will at once do full justice according to the laws of Wales and the said regions.

(58) We will at once returned the son of Llewelyn, all Welsh hostages, and the charters delivered to us as security for the peace.

(59) With regard to the return of the sisters and hostages of Alexander, king of Scotland, his liberties and his rights, we will treat him in the same way as our other barons of England, unless it appears from the charters that we hold from his father William, formerly King of Scotland, that he should be treated otherwise. This matter shall be resolved by the judgement of his equals in our court.

(60) All these customs and liberties that we have granted shall be observed in our kingdom in so far as concerns our own relations with our subjects. Let all men of our kingdom, whether clergy or laymen, observe them similarly in their relations with their own men.

(61) Since we have granted all these things for God, for the better ordering of our kingdom, and to allay the discord that has arisen between us and our barons, and since we desire that they shall be enjoyed in their entirety, with lasting strength, for ever, we give and grant to the barons the following security:

The barons shall elect twenty-five of their number to keep, and cause to be observed with all their might, the peace and liberties granted and confirmed to them by this charter.

If we, our chief justice, our officials, or any of our servants offend in any respect against any man, or transgress any of the articles of the peace or of this security, and the offence is made known to four of the said twenty-five barons, they shall come to us – or in our absence from the kingdom to the chief justice – to declare it and claim immediate redress. If we, or in our absence abroad the chief justice, make no redress within forty days, reckoning from the day on which the offence was declared to us or to him, the four barons shall refer the matter to the rest of the twenty-five barons, who may distrain upon and assail us in every way possible, with the support of the whole community of the land, by seizing our castles, lands, possessions, or anything else saving only our person and those of the queen and our children, until they have secured such redress as they have determined upon. Having secured the redress, they may then resume their normal obedience to us.

Any man who so desires may take an oath to obey the commands of the twenty-five barons for the achievement of these ends, and to join with them in assailing us to the utmost of his power. We give public and free permission to take this oath to any man who so desires, and that no time will we prohibit any man from taking it. Indeed, we will compel any of our subjects who are unwilling to take it or swear it at our command.

If one of the twenty-five barons dies or leaves the country, or is prevented in any other way from discharging his duties, the rest of them shall choose another baron in his place, at their discretion, who shall be duly sworn in as they were.

In the event of disagreement among the twenty-five Barons on any matter referred to them for decision, the verdict of the majority present shall have the same validity as the unanimous verdict of the whole twenty-five, whether these were all present or some of those summoned were unwilling or unable to appear.

The twenty-five barons shall swear to obey all the above articles faithfully, and shall cause them to be obeyed by others to the best of their power.

We will not seek to procure from anyone, either by our own efforts or those of a third party, anything by which any part of these concessions or liberties might be revoked or diminished. Should such a thing be procured, it shall be null and void and we will in no time make use of it, either ourselves or through a third party.

(62) We have remitted and pardoned fully to all men any ill-will, hurt, or grudges that have arisen between us and our subjects, whether clergy or laymen, since the beginning of the dispute. We have in addition remitted fully, and for our own part have also pardoned, to all clergy and laymen any offences committed as a result of the said

dispute between Easter in the sixteenth year of our reign (i.e. 1215) and the restoration of peace.

In addition we have caused letters patent to be made for the barons, bearing witness to this security and to the concessions set out above, over the seals of Stephen archbishop of Canterbury, Henry archbishop of Dublin, the other bishops named above, and Master Pandulf.

(63) IT IS ACCORDINGLY OUR WISH AND COMMAND that the English Church shall be free, and that men in our kingdom shall have and keep all these liberties, rights, and concessions, well and peaceably in their fullness and entirety for them and their heirs, of us and our heirs, in all things and all places for ever.

Both we and the barons have sworn that all this shall be observed in good faith and without deceit. Witness the above-mentioned people and many others.

Given by our hand in the meadow that is called Runnymede, between Windsor and Staines, on the fifteenth day of June in the seventeenth year of our reign (i.e. 1215: the new regnal year began on 28 May).

Connect with the author online:

Blog: http://www.annmariethomas.me.uk/
Twitter: @AnnMThomas80
Email: amt.tetelestai@gmail.com
Amazon: amazon.com/author/annmariethomas
Google+:https://plus.google.com/u/0/1018772005
71860215257/about
LinkedIn: http://www.linkedin.com/pub/ann-thomas/56/6b4/193
GoodReads:http://www.goodreads.com/author/show/5827065.Ann_
Marie_Thomas
Shelfari: http://www.shelfari.com/annmariethomas
Facebook: https://www.facebook.com/pages/Alina-The-White-Lady-
of-Oystermouth/160902344026965

If you enjoy this book, try my stories of medieval Gower:

Alina, The White Lady of Oystermouth. The story of how a little rebellion by the heir to Gower ended up toppling Edward II from the English throne.
Print book & Kindle version available on Amazon
UK: http://amzn.to/lq7XKS
Kindle from Amazon US: http://amzn.to/1gjc32x

Broken Reed: The Lords of Gower and King John. The rise and fall of the greatest of the de Breoses, William, 4th Lord of Bramber, Lord of Gower and many other lands besides. Covered in *The Magna Carta Story*, this is the full story from a Gower perspective.
Print book & Kindle version available on Amazon
UK: http://amzn.to/1c9dRuf
Kindle from Amazon US:
http://www.amazon.com/dp/B00EU8SKPK

Both illustrated by the same talented artist, Carrie Francis.

38623915R00034

Printed in Poland
by Amazon Fulfillment
Poland Sp. z o.o., Wrocław